WHY DO ANIMALS HAVE

PAWS and CLAWS

Elizabeth Miles

Heinemann LIBRARY

www.heinemann.co.uk/library
Visit our website to find out more information about **Heinemann Library** books.

To order:
 Phone 44 (0) 1865 888066
 Send a fax to 44 (0) 1865 314091
 Visit the Heinemann Bookshop at www.heinemann.co.uk/library to browse our catalogue and order online.

First published in Great Britain by Heinemann Library, Halley Court, Jordan Hill, Oxford
OX2 8EJ, a division of Reed Educational and Professional Publishing Ltd. Heinemann is a registered trademark of Reed Educational & Professional Publishing Limited.

OXFORD MELBOURNE AUCKLAND JOHANNESBURG BLANTYRE
GABORONE IBADAN PORTSMOUTH NH (USA) CHICAGO

Designed by David Oakley@Arnos Design
Originated by Dot Gradations
Printed in Hong Kong.

ISBN 0 431 15322 1
06 05 04 03 02
10 9 8 7 6 5 4 3 2 1

British Library Cataloguing in Publication Data

Miles, Elizabeth
  Why do animals have paws and claws
  1.Hand - Juvenile literature 2.claws - Juvenile literature
  3.Physiology - Juvenile literature
  I.Title
  573.9'98'1

Acknowledgements
The Publishers would like to thank the following for permission to reproduce photographs: BBC NHU/Pete Oxford p. 28; BBC NHU/Anup Shah p. 17; BBC NHU/Jeff Foot p. 25; BBC NHU/Miles Barton p. 22; Bruce Coleman p. 26; Bruce Coleman /Pacific Stock p. 29; Bruce Coleman/John Shaw p. 5; Corbis pp. 6, 23, 27; digital vision pp. 7, 8, 13, 30; Imagebank p. 4; NHPA/Patrick Fagot p. 15; NHPA/T. Kitchin and V. Hurst p. 11; NHPA/Daniel Heuclin pp. 16, 19; NHPA/Nigel J Dennis p. 10; NHPA/Steve Robinson p. 24; NHPA/Yves Lanceau p. 18; Oxford Scientific Films/David Haring p. 20; Oxford Scientific Films/Alan G Nelson p. 21; Oxford Scientific Films/Zig Leszczynski p. 9; Tony Stone/Lori Adamski Peek p. 12; Warren Photographic p. 14.

Cover photograph reproduced with permission of Bruce Coleman.

Our thanks to Claire Robinson, Head of Visitor Information and Education at London Zoo, for her help in the preparation of this book.

Every effort has been made to contact copyright holders of any material reproduced in this book. Any omissions will be rectified in subsequent printings if notice is given to the Publisher.

Contents

Words in bold, **like this**, are explained in the Glossary.

Why do animals have hands and paws?

We use our hands all the time. We use them to hold, catch and grasp all kinds of things. We grasp pens and pencils, we hold our school bags and we catch balls.

We have hands at the end of our arms, but many animals don't. A bear has paws instead of hands. Bears use their paws to catch fish from the river.

Fingers and thumbs

Monkeys and apes are **primates**. They have fingers and thumbs on their hands, just as we do. Fingers and thumbs have **joints**, so they bend easily.

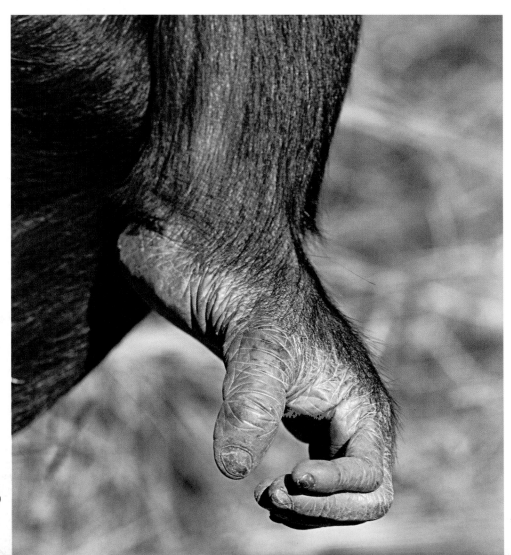

To grip the branch, an orang-utan wraps its thumb one way round the branch, and its fingers round the other way. Fingernails protect the tips of its fingers and thumbs.

Paws

A panda has paws. Paws have claws instead of fingernails. Each of the panda's paws has six short **digits**. A panda uses its front paws to hold **bamboo** plants so it can eat the leaves.

A chipmunk holds its food with its paws, too. Its long digits grasp nuts and tiny seeds to eat. It also uses its paws to pick up and hide food, ready to eat later.

Pads

Paws have spongy **pads** underneath for the animal to walk on. A lion's pads help it to walk very quietly when it is creeping up on its **prey**.

A puma's tough, spongy pads help to protect
its paws. Its paws do not get cut by rocks
and stones. When the puma leaps, the pads
give it a softer landing.

Blunt claws and sharp claws

Paws always have claws. Some animal claws are **blunt** and some are sharp. A dog's claws are quite blunt. If a dog jumps up, it rarely scratches anyone.

A koala has sharp claws for climbing trees. It stays in the trees for most of the time. It digs its claws into the **bark** of the tree for a firm grip.

Hidden claws

Claws are sometimes hidden inside an animal's paws. A cat keeps its claws hidden most of the time. This keeps them sharp. It uses its claws to catch things and to climb.

Tigers are a type of wild cat. They have sharp, curved claws. These spring out to catch the tiger's **prey**. Tigers also use their sharp claws when they scratch trees. This warns other tigers to stay away.

Thick claws

A **sloth** has thick, curved claws. The sloth hooks them over a branch and moves slowly along, upside down. Sloths hang by their claws when they sleep.

An anteater has thick, curved claws. It uses its strong, sharp claws to rip open **termite** mounds. The anteater walks on the outside of its paws to stop its claws becoming **blunt**.

Crushing claws

Some animals have very strong, crushing claws. A lobster lives on the sea floor. It uses its front claws to catch and crush its **prey**. Its claws are called pincers.

A scorpion has large front claws called pincers, too. It uses them to grab and crush its prey. The pincers have two parts that open and close together like scissors.

Special fingers

Some animals have special fingers for special jobs. An aye-aye is like a monkey. It has a very long middle finger. It pushes this finger into the **bark** of a tree to pull out **grubs**.

A tarsier is like a tiny monkey. It has flat, **padded** fingertips and long fingernails. It jumps from branch to branch in trees, catching insects to eat. It needs to grip the tree firmly.

Clever hands and paws

Many animals can do all kinds of things with their hands or paws. A macaque is another type of monkey. It carries food in its hands to a river. Then it uses its hands to wash the food in the water.

Racoons use their paws when they look for food. Sometimes they come near people's houses and look through rubbish, too.

Hands and paws for holding tools

A chimpanzee can use tools. It holds a stick in its hands and uses it to catch **termites**. It pushes the stick into the termite nest and eats the termites it pulls out.

A sea otter gathers **clams** and a stone in its paws. It uses the stone as a tool for cracking open the shell. Then it eats the clam inside.

Digging paws

Some animals have special paws to help them get around where they live. A mole lives underground. Its front paws and long claws can dig tunnels through the soil.

This grizzly bear has strong paws with long fingernails. It uses its paws to dig up food to eat. Here it is digging **clams** on a beach.

Look, no hands!

Some animals grasp things without hands or paws. A boa is a snake that coils its strong body round a tree to hold on. It squeezes its **prey** like this, too.

An octopus has **tentacles** and suckers to
hold and grasp. The tentacles catch its prey.
The round suckers stick to the prey and
stop it from escaping.

Fact file

This baby racoon is using its claws to cling on to the pole.

- Many animals, have claws. **Primates** have fingernails instead.

- Fish do not have hands or paws. They have flippers and fins instead.

- Paws can be soft and safe. Some animals, like cats, use their paws to cover their eyes when they go to sleep. They also wash their face with their paws.

- The pads on the paws of a wild cat, like a cheetah, have ridges. The ridges are like the tread on a car tyre and stop the cat from slipping.

Glossary

bamboo   plant with hollow stem. Pandas eat only bamboo.

bark   strong outside part of a tree trunk or branch

blunt   not sharp

clam   type of animal that lives in a shell underwater

digits   fingers or toes

flippers   arm-like parts of an animal that help it to swim

grubs   insects that are not fully grown

joints   places in the body where it can bend. A finger has several joints.

pads   soft spongy parts of a paw

prey   animals hunted as food

primates   animals such as orang-utan, monkeys, apes and also people. All primates have hands with fingers and thumbs.

sloth   hairy animal that hangs upside down in trees

tentacles   long arm-like body parts that stick out from an octopus

termites   insects that live in large groups in mounds

Index

Titles in the *Why Do Animals Have* series include:

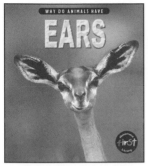

Hardback 0431 15311 6

Hardback 0431 15310 8

Hardback 0431 15326 4

Hardback 0431 15323 X

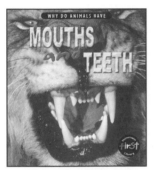

Hardback 0431 15314 0

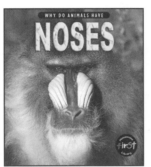

Hardback 0431 15312 4

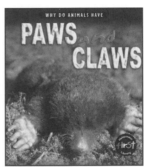

Hardback 0431 15322 1

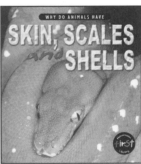

Hardback 0431 15325 6

Hardback 0431 15313 2

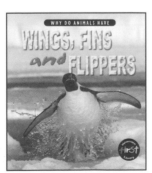

Hardback 0431 15324 8

Find out about the other titles in this series on our website www.heinemann.co.uk/library